The Elder Statesman

The Elder Statesman

a play by

T. S. ELIOT

Farrar, Straus and Cudahy, New York

Library of Congress Catalog Number: 59-6590
Manufactured in the United States of America
by American Book–Stratford Press, Inc., New York

TO MY WIFE

To whom I owe the leaping delight
That quickens my senses in our wakingtime
And the rhythm that governs the repose of our sleepingtime,
   The breathing in unison

Of lovers . . .
Who think the same thoughts without need of speech
And babble the same speech without need of meaning:

To you I dedicate this book, to return as best I can
With words a little part of what you have given me.
The words mean what they say, but some have a further meaning
   For you and me only.

I WISH to thank all those who have assisted me by suggestions and criticisms of this play at various stages of its development, and to make special acknowledgment to the following: to Mr. John Hayward, whose criticism of the first draft of the first act led to its reconstruction; to Mr. T. C. Worsley for a hint in a critical notice of the Edinburgh production which inspired Mr. Martin Browne to propose a small but important excision; to Mr. Henry Sherek and Mr. Browne for criticism and encouragement throughout, and to Mr. Browne for his labours in assisting me to condense, expand and reorganise; to my wife who in the course of typing the several drafts of the play, helped me to improve details.

T. S. E.

November 1958

Characters

MONICA CLAVERTON-FERRY
CHARLES HEMINGTON
LAMBERT
LORD CLAVERTON
FEDERICO GOMEZ
MRS. PIGGOTT
MRS. CARGHILL
MICHAEL CLAVERTON-FERRY

ACT I

The drawing-room of Lord Claverton's London house.
Four o'clock in the afternoon.

ACT II

The Terrace at Badgley Court. Morning.

ACT III

The Same. Late afternoon of the following day.

Act One

The drawing-room of LORD CLAVERTON'S *London house.*
Four o'clock in the afternoon.
[*Voices in the hall*]

CHARLES

Is your father at home to-day?

MONICA

You'll see him at tea.

CHARLES

But if I'm not going to have you to myself
There's really no point in my staying to tea.
[*Enter* MONICA *and* CHARLES *carrying parcels*]

MONICA

But you *must* stay to tea. That was understood
When you said you could give me the whole afternoon.

CHARLES

But I couldn't say what I wanted to say to you
Over luncheon . . .

11

MONICA

That's your own fault.
You should have taken me to some other restaurant
Instead of to one where the *maître d'hôtel*
And the waiters all seem to be your intimate friends.

CHARLES

It's the only place where I'm really well known
And get well served. And when *you're* with me
It must be a perfect lunch.

MONICA

It was a perfect lunch.
But I know what men are—they like to show off.
That's masculine vanity, to want to have the waiters
All buzzing round you: and it reminds the girl
That she's not the only one who's been there with him.

CHARLES

Well, tease me if you like. But a man does feel a fool
If he takes you to a place where he's utterly unknown
And the waiters all appear to be avoiding his eye.

MONICA

We're getting off the point . . .

CHARLES

You've got me off *my* point . . .
I was trying to explain . . .

12

MONICA

It's simply the question
Of your staying to tea. As you practically promised.

CHARLES

What you don't understand is that I have a grievance.
On Monday you're leaving London, with your father:
I arranged to be free for the whole afternoon
On the plain understanding . . .

MONICA

That you should stop to tea.

CHARLES

When I said that I was free for the whole afternoon,
That meant you were to give *me* the whole afternoon.
I couldn't say what I wanted to, in a restaurant;
And then you took me on a shopping expedition . . .

MONICA

If you don't like shopping with me . . .

CHARLES

Of course I like shopping with you.
But how can one *talk* on a shopping expedition—
Except to guess what you want to buy
And advise you to buy it.

MONICA

But why not stop to tea?

13

CHARLES

Very well then, I will stop to tea,
But you know I won't get a chance to talk to you.
You know that. Now that your father's retired
He's at home every day. And you're leaving London.
And because your father simply can't bear it
That any man but he should have you to himself,
Before I've said two words he'll come ambling in . . .

MONICA

You've said a good deal more than two words already.
And besides, my father doesn't amble.
You're not at all respectful.

CHARLES

                  I try to be respectful;
But you know that I shan't have a minute alone with
    you.

MONICA

You've already had several minutes alone with me
Which you've wasted in wrangling. But seriously,
    Charles,
Father's sure to be buried in the library
And he won't think of leaving it until he's called for tea.
So why not talk now? Though I know very well
What it is you want to say. I've heard it all before.

14

CHARLES

And you'll hear it again. You think I'm going to tell you
Once more, that I'm in love with you. Well, you're right.
But I've something else to say that I haven't said before,
That will give you a shock. I believe *you* love *me*.

MONICA

Oh, what a dominating man you are!
Really, you must imagine you're a hypnotist.

CHARLES

Is this a time to torment me? But I'm selfish
In saying that, because I think—
I think you're tormenting yourself as well.

MONICA

You're right. I am. Because *I am* in love with you.

CHARLES

So I was right! The moment I'd said it
I was badly frightened. For I didn't *know* you loved me—
I merely wanted to believe it. And I've made you say so!
But now that you've said so, you must say it again,
For I need so much assurance! Are you sure you're not
    mistaken?

MONICA

How did this come, Charles? It crept so softly
On silent feet, and stood behind my back
Quietly, a long time, a long long time
Before I felt its presence.

CHARLES

        Your words seem to come
From very far away. Yet very near. You are changing me
And I am changing you.

MONICA

        Already
How much of me is you?

CHARLES

        And how much of me is you?
I'm not the same person as a moment ago.
What do the words mean now—*I* and *you?*

MONICA

In our private world—now we have our private world—
The meanings are different. Look! We're back in the
    room
That we entered only a few minutes ago.
Here's an armchair, there's the table;
There's the door . . . and I hear someone coming:
It's Lambert with the tea . . .
[*Enter* LAMBERT *with trolley*]
        and I shall say, "Lambert,
Please let his lordship know the tea is waiting."

LAMBERT

Yes, Miss Monica.

16

MONICA

I'm very glad, Charles,
That you *can* stay to tea.

[*Exit* LAMBERT]

—Now we're in the public world.

CHARLES

And your father will come. With his calm possessive air
And his kindly welcome, which is always a reminder
That I mustn't stay too long, for you belong to him.
He seems so placidly to take it for granted
That you don't really care for any company but his!

MONICA

You're not to assume that anything I've said to you
Has given you the right to criticise my father.
In the first place, you don't understand him;
In the second place, we're not engaged yet.

CHARLES

Aren't we? We're agreed that we're in love with each
    other,
And, there being no legal impediment
Isn't that enough to constitute an engagement?
Aren't you sure that you want to marry me?

MONICA

Yes, Charles. I'm sure that I want to marry you
When I'm free to do so. But by that time
You may have changed your mind. Such things have
    happened.

17

CHARLES

That won't happen to me.

[*Knock. Enter* LAMBERT]

LAMBERT

Excuse me, Miss Monica. His Lordship said to tell you
Not to wait tea for him.

MONICA

Thank you, Lambert.

LAMBERT

He's busy at the moment. But he won't be very long.

[*Exit*]

CHARLES

Don't you understand that you're torturing me?
How long will you be imprisoned, alone with your
    father
In that very expensive hotel for convalescents
To which you're taking him? And what after that?

MONICA

There are several good reasons why I should go with
    him.

CHARLES

Better reasons than for marrying me?
What reasons?

18

MONICA

First, his terror of being alone.
In the life he's led, he's never had to be alone.
And when he's been at home in the evening,
Even when he's reading, or busy with his papers,
He needs to have someone else in the room with him,
Reading too—or just sitting—someone
Not occupied with anything that can't be interrupted.
Someone to make a remark to now and then.
And mostly it's been me.

CHARLES

I know it's been you.
It's a pity that you haven't had brothers and sisters
To share the burden. Sisters, I should say,
For your brother's never been of any use to you.

MONICA

And never will be of any use to anybody,
I'm afraid. Poor Michael! Mother spoilt him
And Father was too severe—so they're always at logger-
heads.

CHARLES

But you spoke of several reasons for your going with
your father.
Is there any better reason than his fear of solitude?

MONICA

The second reason is exactly the opposite:
It's his fear of being exposed to strangers.

CHARLES

But he's most alive when he's among people
Managing, manoeuvring, cajoling or bullying—
At all of which he's a master. Strangers!

MONICA

You don't understand. It's one thing meeting people
When you're in authority, with authority's costume,
When the man that people see when they meet you
Is not the private man, but the public personage.
In politics Father wore a public label.
And later, as chairman of public companies,
Always his privacy has been preserved.

CHARLES

His privacy has been so well preserved
That I've sometimes wondered whether there was
    any . . .
Private self to preserve.

MONICA

              There *is* a private self, Charles.
I'm sure of that.

CHARLES

           You've given two reasons,
One the contradiction of the other.
Can there be a third?

MONICA

The third reason is this:
I've only just been given it by Dr. Selby—
Father is much iller than he is aware of:
It may be, he will never return from Badgley Court.
But Selby wants him to have every encouragement—
If he's hopeful, he's likely to live a little longer.
That's why Selby chose the place. A *convalescent* home
With the atmosphere of an hotel—
Nothing about it to suggest the clinic—
Every thing about it to suggest recovery.

CHARLES

This is your best reason, and the most depressing;
For this situation may persist for a long time,
And you'll go on postponing and postponing our mar-
    riage.

MONICA

I'm afraid . . . not a very long time, Charles.
It's almost certain that the winter in Jamaica
Will never take place. "Make the reservations,"
Selby said, "as if you were going."
But Badgley Court's so near your constituency!
You can come down at weekends, even when the House
    is sitting.
And you can take me out, if Father can spare me.
But he'll simply love having you to talk to!

CHARLES

I know he's used to seeing me about.

21

MONICA

I've seen him looking at you. He was thinking of himself
When he was your age—when he started like you,
With the same hopes, the same ambitions—
And of his disappointments.

CHARLES

                                 Is that wistfulness,
Compassion, or . . . envy?

MONICA

                                Envy is everywhere.
Who is without envy? And most people
Are unaware or unashamed of being envious.
It's all we can ask if compassion and wistfulness . . .
And tenderness, Charles! Are mixed with envy:
I do believe that he is fond of you.
So you must come often. And oh, Charles dear—
[*Enter* LORD CLAVERTON]

MONICA

You've been very long in coming, Father. What have you
    been doing?

LORD CLAVERTON

Good afternoon, Charles. You might have guessed,
    Monica,
What I've been doing. Don't you recognise this book?

MONICA

It's your engagement book.

LORD CLAVERTON

Yes, I've been brooding over it.

MONICA

But what a time for your engagement book!
You know what the doctors said: complete relaxation
And to think about nothing. Though I know that won't
be easy.

LORD CLAVERTON

That is just what I was doing.

MONICA

Thinking of nothing?

LORD CLAVERTON

Contemplating nothingness. Just remember:
Every day, year after year, over my breakfast,
I have looked at this book—or one just like it—
You know I keep the old ones on a shelf together;
I could look in the right book, and find out what I was
doing
Twenty years ago, to-day, at this hour of the afternoon.
If I've been looking at this engagement book, to-day,
Not over breakfast, but before tea,
It's the empty pages that I've been fingering—
The first empty pages since I entered Parliament.
I used to jot down notes of what I had to say to people:
Now I've no more to say, and no one to say it to.
I've been wondering . . . how many more empty pages?

MONICA

You would soon fill them up if we allowed you to!
That's my business to prevent. You know I'm to protect
   you
From your own restless energy—the inexhaustible
Sources of the power that wears out the machine.

LORD CLAVERTON

They've dried up, Monica, and you know it.
They talk of rest, these doctors, Charles; they tell me to
   be cautious,
To take life easily. Take life easily!
It's like telling a man he mustn't run for trains
When the last thing he wants is to take a train for any-
   where!
No, I've not the slightest longing for the life I've left—
Only fear of the emptiness before me.
If I had the energy to work myself to death
How gladly would I face death! But waiting, simply
   waiting,
With no desire to act, yet a loathing of inaction.
A fear of the vacuum, and no desire to fill it.
It's just like sitting in an empty waiting room
In a railway station on a branch line,
After the last train, after all the other passengers
Have left, and the booking office is closed
And the porters have gone. What am I waiting for
In a cold and empty room before an empty grate?
For no one. For nothing.

MONICA

                    Yet you've been looking forward
To this very time! You know how you grumbled
At the farewell banquet, with the tributes from the staff,
The presentation, and the speech you had to make
And the speeches that you had to listen to!

LORD CLAVERTON

          [*pointing to a silver salver, still lying in its case*]
I don't know which impressed me more, the insincerity
Of what was said about me, or of my reply—
All to thank them for that.
                    O the grudging contributions
That bought this piece of silver! The inadequate levy
That made the Chairman's Price! And my fellow direc-
    tors
Saying "we must put our hands in our pockets
To double this collection—it must be something showy."
This would do for visiting cards—if people still left cards
And if I was going to have any visitors.

MONICA

Father, you simply want to revel in gloom!
You know you've retired in a blaze of glory—
You've read every word about you in the papers.

CHARLES

And the leading articles saying "we are confident
That his sagacious counsel will long continue
To be at the disposal of the Government in power."

And the expectation that your voice will be heard
In debate in the Upper House . . .

LORD CLAVERTON

The established liturgy
Of the Press on any conspicuous retirement.
My obituary, if I had died in harness,
Would have occupied a column and a half
With an inset, a portrait taken twenty years ago.
In five years' time, it will be the half of that;
In ten years' time, a paragraph.

CHARLES

That's the reward
Of every public man.

LORD CLAVERTON

Say rather, the exequies
Of the failed successes, the successful failures,
Who occupy positions that other men covet.
When we go, a good many folk are mildly grieved,
And our closest associates, the small minority
Of those who really understand the place we filled
Are inwardly delighted. They won't want my ghost
Walking in the City or sitting in the Lords.
And I, who recognise myself as a ghost
Shan't want to be seen there. It makes me smile
To think that men should be frightened of ghosts.
If they only knew how frightened a ghost can be of men!
[*Knock. Enter* LAMBERT]

26

Excuse me, My Lord. There's a gentleman downstairs
Is very insistent that he must see you.
I told him you never saw anyone, My Lord,
But by previous appointment. He said he knew that,
So he had brought this note. He said that when you read
     it
You would want to see him. Said you'd be very angry
If you heard that he'd gone away without your seeing
     him.

LORD CLAVERTON

What sort of a person?

LAMBERT

                          A foreign person
By the looks of him. But talks good English.
A pleasant-spoken gentleman.

LORD CLAVERTON

[*after reading the note*]
                          I'll see him in the library.
No, stop. I've left too many papers about there.
I'd better see him here.

LAMBERT

                 Very good, My Lord.
Shall I take the trolley, Miss Monica?

MONICA

Yes, thank you, Lambert.   [*Exit* LAMBERT]

27

CHARLES

I ought to be going.

MONICA

Let *us* go into the library. And then I'll see you off.

LORD CLAVERTON

I'm sorry to turn you out of the room like this,
But I'll have to see this man by myself, Monica.
I've never heard of this Señor Gomez
But he comes with a letter of introduction
From a man I used to know. I can't refuse to see him.
Though from what I remember of the man who intro-
    duces him
I expect he wants money. Or to sell me something
    worthless.

MONICA

You ought not to bother with such people now, Father.
If you haven't got rid of him in twenty minutes
I'll send Lambert to tell you that you have to take a
    trunk call.
Come, Charles. Will you bring my coat?

CHARLES

                    I'll say goodbye, sir.
And look forward to seeing you both at Badgley Court
In a week or two.
[*Enter* LAMBERT]

LAMBERT
Mr. Gomez, My Lord.

LORD CLAVERTON
Goodbye, Charles. And please remember
That we both want to see you, whenever you can come
If you're in the vicinity. Don't we, Monica?

MONICA
Yes, Father. (*To* CHARLES) We *both* want to see you.
[*Exeunt* MONICA *and* CHARLES]
[LAMBERT *shows in* GOMEZ]

LORD CLAVERTON
Good evening, Mr. . . . Gomez. You're a friend of Mr.
Culverwell?

GOMEZ
We're as thick as thieves, you might almost say.
Don't you know me, Dick?

LORD CLAVERTON
Fred Culverwell!
Why do you come back with another name?

GOMEZ
You've changed your name too, since I knew you.
When we were up at Oxford, you were plain Dick Ferry.
Then, when you married, you took your wife's name
And became Mr. Richard Claverton-Ferry;

29

And finally, Lord Claverton. I've followed your example,
And done the same, in a modest way.
You know, where *I* live, people do change their names;
And besides, my wife's name is a good deal more normal
In my country, than Culverwell—and easier to pro-
nounce.

LORD CLAVERTON

Have you lived out there ever since . . . you left England?

GOMEZ

Ever since I finished my sentence.

LORD CLAVERTON

What has brought you to England?

GOMEZ

Call it homesickness,
Curiosity, restlessness, whatever you like.
But I've been a pretty hard worker all these years
And I thought, now's the time to take a long holiday,
Let's say a rest cure—that's what I've come for.
You see, I'm a widower, like you, Dick.
So I'm pretty footloose. Gomez, you see,
Is now a highly respected citizen
Of a Central American republic: San Marco.
It's as hard to become a respected citizen
Out there, as it is here. With this qualification:
Out there they respect you for rather different reasons.

30

LORD CLAVERTON

Do you mean that you've won respect out there
By the sort of activity that lost you respect
Here in England?

GOMEZ

Not at all, not at all.
I think that was rather an unkind suggestion.
I've always kept on the right side of the law—
And seen that the law turned its right side to *me*.
Sometimes I've had to pay pretty heavily;
But I learnt by experience whom to pay;
And a little money laid out in the right manner
In the right places, pays many times over.
I assure you it does.

LORD CLAVERTON

In other words
You have been engaged in systematic corruption.

GOMEZ

No, Dick, there's a fault in your logic.
How can one corrupt those who are already corrupted?
I can swear that I've never corrupted anybody.
In fact, I've never come across an official
Innocent enough to be corruptible.

LORD CLAVERTON

It would seem then that most of your business
Has been of such a nature that, if carried on in England,
It might land you in gaol again?

GOMEZ

That's true enough,
Except for a false inference. I wouldn't dream
Of carrying on such business if I lived in England.
I have the same standards of morality
As the society in which I find myself.
I do nothing in England that you would disapprove of.

LORD CLAVERTON

That's something, at least, to be thankful for.
I trust you've no need to engage in forgery.

GOMEZ

Forgery, Dick? An absurd suggestion!
Forgery, I can tell you, is a mug's game.
I say that—with conviction.
No, forgery, or washing cheques, or anything of that
    nature,
Is certain to be found out sooner or later.
And then what happens? You have to move on.
That wouldn't do for me. I'm too domestic.
And by the way, I've several children,
All grown up, doing well for themselves.
I wouldn't allow either of my sons
To go into politics. In my country, Dick,
Politicians can't afford mistakes. The prudent ones
Always have an aeroplane ready:
And keep an account in a bank in Switzerland.
The ones who don't get out in time
Find themselves in gaol and not very comfortable,

Or before a firing squad.

You don't know what serious politics is like!

I said to my boys: "Never touch politics.

Stay out of politics, and play both parties:

What you don't get from one you may get from the
    other."

Dick, don't tell me that there isn't any whisky in the
    house?

LORD CLAVERTON

I can provide whisky. [*Presses the bell*]
               But why have you come?

GOMEZ

             You've asked me that already!

To see you, Dick, a natural desire!

For you're the only old friend I can trust.

LORD CLAVERTON

You really trust me? I appreciate the compliment.

GOMEZ

Which you're sure you deserve. But when I say
    "trust". . .

[*Knock. Enter* LAMBERT]

LORD CLAVERTON

Lambert, will you bring in the whisky. And soda.

LAMBERT

Very good, My Lord.

33

GOMEZ

And some ice.

LAMBERT

Ice? Yes, My Lord.

[*Exit*]

GOMEZ

I began to say: when I say "trust"
I use the term as experience has taught me.
It's nonsense to talk of trusting people
In general. What does that mean? One trusts a man
Or a woman—in this respect or that.
A won't let me down in this relationship,
B won't let me down in some other connection.
But, as I've always said to my boys:
"When you come to the point where you need to trust
    someone
You must make it worth his while to be trustworthy."
[*During this* LAMBERT *enters silently, deposits tray and
    exit.*]

LORD CLAVERTON

Won't you help yourself?
            [GOMEZ *does so, liberally*]

GOMEZ

            And what about you?

LORD CLAVERTON

I don't take it, thank you.

34

GOMEZ

A reformed character!

LORD CLAVERTON

I should like to know why you need to trust *me*.

GOMEZ

That's perfectly simple. I come back to England
After thirty-five years. Can you imagine
What it would be like to have been away from home
For thirty-five years? I was twenty-five—
The same age as you—when I went away,
Thousands of miles away, to another climate,
To another language, other standards of behaviour,
To fabricate for myself another personality
And to take another name. Think what that means—
To take another name.
                [*Gets up and helps himself to whisky*]
                        But of course you know!
Just enough to think you know more than you do.
You've changed your name twice—by easy stages,
And each step was merely a step up the ladder,
So you weren't aware of becoming a different person:
But where *I* changed my name, there was no social
        ladder.
It was jumping a gap—and you can't jump back again.
I parted from myself by a sudden effort,
You, so slowly and sweetly, that you've never woken up
To the fact that Dick Ferry died long ago.
I married a girl who didn't know a word of English,

Didn't want to learn English, wasn't interested
In anything that happened four thousand miles away,
Only believed what the parish priest told her.
I made my children learn English—it's useful;
I always talk to them in English.
But do they think in English? No, they do not.
They think in Spanish, but their thoughts are Indian
    thoughts.
O God, Dick, *you* don't know what it's like
To be so cut off! Homesickness!
Homesickness is a sickly word.
You don't understand such isolation
As mine, you think you do . . .

LORD CLAVERTON

                I'm sure I do,
I've always been alone.

GOMEZ

          Oh, loneliness—
Everybody knows what that's like.
Your loneliness—so cosy, warm and padded:
You're not isolated—merely insulated.
It's only when you come to see that you have lost *your-
    self*
That you are quite alone.

LORD CLAVERTON

              I'm waiting to hear
Why you should need to trust me.

GOMEZ

Perfectly simple.
My father's dead long since—that's a good thing.
My mother—I dare say she's still alive.
But she must be very old. And she must think I'm dead;
And as for my married sisters—I don't suppose their husbands
Were ever told the story. *They* wouldn't want to see me.
No, I need one old friend, a friend whom I can trust—
And one who will accept both Culverwell and Gomez—
See Culverwell as Gomez—Gomez as Culverwell.
I need you, Dick, to give me reality!

LORD CLAVERTON

But according to the description you have given
Of trusting people, how do you propose
To make it worth my while to be trustworthy?

GOMEZ

It's done already, Dick; done many years ago:
Adoption tried, and grappled to my soul
With hoops of steel, and all that sort of thing.
We'll come to that, very soon. Isn't it strange
That there should always have been this bond between us?

LORD CLAVERTON

It has never crossed my mind. Develop the point.

GOMEZ

Well, consider what we were when we went up to
    Oxford
And then what I became under your influence.

LORD CLAVERTON

You cannot attribute your . . . misfortune to *my*
    influence.

GOMEZ

I was just about as different as anyone could be
From the sort of men you'd been at school with—
I didn't fit in to your set, and I knew it.
When you started to take me up at Oxford
I've no doubt your friends wondered what you found in
    me—
A scholarship boy from an unknown grammar school.
I didn't know either, but I was flattered.
Later, I came to understand: you made friends with me
Because it flattered *you*—tickled your love of power
To see that I was flattered, and that I admired you.
Everyone expected that I should get a First.
I suppose your tutor thought you'd be sent down.
It went the other way. You stayed the course, at least.
I had plenty of time to think things over, later.

LORD CLAVERTON

And what is the conclusion that you came to?

GOMEZ

This is how it worked out, Dick. You liked to play the
    rake,
But you never went too far. There's a prudent devil
Inside you, Dick. He never came to *my* help.

LORD CLAVERTON

I certainly admit no responsibility,
None whatever, for what happened to you later.

GOMEZ

You led me on at Oxford, and left me to it.
And so it came about that I was sent down
With the consequences which you remember:
A miserable clerkship—which your father found for me,
And expensive tastes—which you had fostered in me,
And, equally unfortunate, a talent for penmanship.
Hence, as you have just reminded me
Defalcation and forgery. And then my stretch
Which gave me time to think it all out.

LORD CLAVERTON

That's the second time you have mentioned your re-
    flections.
But there's just one thing you seem to have forgotten:
I came to your assistance when you were released.

GOMEZ

Yes, and paid my passage out. I know the reason:
You wanted to get rid of me. I shall tell you why
    presently.

Now let's look for a moment at *your* life history.
You had plenty of money, and you made a good mar-
    riage—
Or so it seemed—and with your father's money
And your wife's family influence, you got on in politics.
Shall we say that you did very well by yourself?
Though not, I suspect, as well as you had hoped.

LORD CLAVERTON

I was never accused of making a mistake.

GOMEZ

No, in England mistakes are anonymous
Because the man who accepts responsibility
Isn't the man who made the mistake.
That's your convention. Or if it's known you made it
You simply get moved to another post
Where at least you can't make quite the same mistake.
At the worst, you go into opposition
And let the other people make mistakes
Until your own have been more or less forgotten.
I dare say you did make some mistake, Dick . . .
That would account for your leaving politics
And taking a conspicuous job in the City
Where the Government could always consult you
But of course didn't have to take your advice . . .
I've made a point, you see, of following your career.

LORD CLAVERTON

I am touched by your interest.

40

GOMEZ

              I have a gift for friendship.
I rejoiced in your success. But one thing has puzzled me.
You were given a ministry before you were fifty:
That should have led you to the very top!
And yet you withdrew from the world of politics
And went into the City. Director of a bank
And chairman of companies. You looked the part—
Cut out to be an impressive figurehead.
But again, you've retired at sixty. Why at sixty?

LORD CLAVERTON

Knowing as much about me as you do
You must have read that I retired at the insistence of my
    doctors.

GOMEZ

Oh yes, the usual euphemism.
And yet I wonder. It *is* surprising:
You should have been good for another five years
At least. Why did they let you retire?

LORD CLAVERTON

If you want to know, I had had a stroke.
And I might have another.

GOMEZ

            Yes. You might have another.
But I wonder what brought about this . . . stroke;
And I wonder whether you're the great economist
And financial wizard that you're supposed to be.

41

And I've learned something of other vicissitudes.
Dick, I was very very sorry when I heard
That your marriage had not been altogether happy.
And as for your son—from what I've heard about *him,*
He's followed your undergraduate career
Without the protection of that prudent devil
Of yours, to tell him not to go too far.
Well, now, I'm beginning to be thirsty again.
[*Pours himself whisky*]

Lord Claverton

An interesting historical epitome.
Though I cannot accept it as altogether accurate.
The only thing I find surprising
In the respected citizen of San Marco
Is that in the midst of the engrossing business
Of the nature of which dark hints have been given,
He's informed himself so carefully about my career.

Gomez

I don't propose to give you a detailed account
Of my own career. I've been very successful.
What would have happened to me, I wonder,
If I had never met you? I should have got my First,
And I might have become the history master
In a school like that from which I went to Oxford.
As it is, I'm somebody—a more important man
In San Marco than I should ever have been in England.

Lord Claverton

So, as you consider yourself a success . . .

GOMEZ

A worldly success, Dick. In another sense
We're both of us failures. But even so,
I'd rather be my kind of failure than yours.

LORD CLAVERTON

And what do you call failure?

GOMEZ

What do I call failure?
The worst kind of failure, in my opinion,
Is the man who has to keep on pretending to himself
That he's a success—the man who in the morning
Has to make up his face before he looks in the mirror.

LORD CLAVERTON

Isn't that the kind of pretence that you're maintaining
In trying to persuade me of your . . . worldly success?

GOMEZ

No, because I know the value of the coinage
I pay myself in.

LORD CLAVERTON

Indeed! How interesting!
I still don't know why you've come to see me
Or what you mean by saying you can trust me.

GOMEZ

Dick, do you remember the moonlight night
We drove back to Oxford? *You* were driving.

Lord Claverton

That happened several times.

Gomez

          One time in particular.
You know quite well to which occasion I'm referring—
A summer night of moonlight and shadows—
The night you ran over the old man in the road.

Lord Claverton

You *said* I ran over an old man in the road.

Gomez

You knew it too. If you had been surprised
When I said "Dick, you've run over somebody"
Wouldn't you have shown it, if only for a second?
You never lifted your foot from the accelerator.

Lord Claverton

We were in a hurry.

Gomez

          More than in a hurry.
You didn't want it to be known where we'd been.
The girls who were with us (what were their names?
I've completely forgotten them) you didn't want *them*
To be called to give evidence. You just couldn't face it.
Do you see now, Dick, why I say I can trust you?

Lord Claverton

If you think that this story would interest the public
Why not sell your version to a Sunday newspaper?

My dear Dick, what a preposterous suggestion!
Who's going to accept the unsupported statement
Of Federico Gomez of San Marco
About something that happened so many years ago?
What damages you'd get! The Press wouldn't look at it.
Besides, you can't think I've any desire
To appear in public as Frederick Culverwell?
No, Dick, your secret's safe with me.
Of course, I might give it to a few friends, in confidence.
It might even reach the ears of some of your acquaint-
    ance—
But you'd never know to whom I'd told it,
Or who knew the story and who didn't. I promise you.
Rely upon me as the soul of discretion.

LORD CLAVERTON

What do you want then? Do you need money?

GOMEZ

My dear chap, you are obtuse!
I said: "Your secret is safe with me,"
And then you . . . well, I'd never have believed
That you would accuse an old friend of . . . blackmail!
On the contrary, I dare say I could buy you out
Several times over. San Marco's a good place
To make money in—though not to *keep* it in.
My investments—not all in my own name either—
Are pretty well spread. For the matter of that,
My current account in Stockholm or Zurich

Would keep me in comfort for the rest of my life.
Really, Dick, you owe me an apology.
Blackmail! On the contrary
Any time you're in a tight corner
My entire resources are at your disposal.
You were a generous friend to me once
As you pointedly reminded me a moment ago.
Now it's my turn, perhaps, to do you a kindness.
[*Enter* LAMBERT]

LAMBERT

Excuse me, My Lord, but Miss Monica asked me
To remind you there's a trunk call coming through for
    you
In five minutes' time.

LORD CLAVERTON

I'll be ready to take it.

[*Exit* LAMBERT]

GOMEZ

Ah, the pre-arranged interruption
To terminate the unwelcome intrusion
Of the visitor in financial distress.
Well, I shan't keep you long, though I dare say your
    caller
Could hang on for another quarter of an hour.

LORD CLAVERTON

Before you go—what is it that you want?

46

GOMEZ

I've been trying to make clear that I only want your
    friendship!
Just as it used to be in the old days
When you taught me expensive tastes. Now it's my turn.
I can have cigars sent direct to you from Cuba
If your doctors allow you a smoke now and then.
I'm a lonely man, Dick, with a craving for affection.
All I want is as much of your company,
So long as I stay here, as I can get.
And the more I get, the longer I may stay.

LORD CLAVERTON

                                This is preposterous!
Do you call it friendship to impose your company
On a man by threats? Why keep up the pretence?

GOMEZ

Threats, Dick! How can you speak of threats?
It's most unkind of you. My only aim
Is to renew our friendship. Don't you understand?

LORD CLAVERTON

I see that when I gave you my friendship
So many years ago, I only gained in return
Your envy, spite and hatred. That is why you attribute
Your downfall to me. But how was I responsible?
We were the same age. You were a free moral agent.
You pretend that I taught you expensive tastes:
If you had not had those tastes already
You would hardly have welcomed my companionship.

47

GOMEZ

Neatly argued, and almost convincing:
Don't you wish you could believe it?

LORD CLAVERTON

                   And what if I decline
To give you the pleasure of my company?

GOMEZ

Oh, I can wait, Dick. You'll relent at last.
You'll come to feel easier when I'm with you
Than when I'm out of sight. You'll be afraid of whispers,
The reflection in the mirror of the face behind you,
The ambiguous smile, the distant salutation,
The sudden silence when you enter the smoking room.
                                  Don't forget, Dick:
You *didn't stop!* Well, I'd better be going.
I hope I haven't outstayed my welcome?
Your telephone pal may be getting impatient.
I'll see you soon again.

LORD CLAVERTON

                 Not very soon, I think.
I am going away.

GOMEZ

             So I've been informed.
I have friends in the press—if not in the peerage.
Good-bye for the present. It's been an elixir
To see you again, and assure myself

That we can begin just where we left off.

[*Exit* GOMEZ]

[LORD CLAVERTON *sits for a few minutes brooding. A knock. Enter* MONICA]

MONICA

Who was it, Father?

LORD CLAVERTON

A man I used to know.

MONICA

Oh, so you knew him?

LORD CLAVERTON

Yes. He'd changed his name.

MONICA

Then I suppose he wanted money?

LORD CLAVERTON

No, he didn't want money.

MONICA

Father, this interview has worn you out.
You must go and rest now, before dinner.

LORD CLAVERTON

Yes, I'll go and rest now. I wish Charles was dining with
  us.
I wish we were having a dinner party.

Father, can't you bear to be alone with me?
If you can't bear to dine alone with me tonight,
What will it be like at Badgley Court?

CURTAIN

Act Two

The terrace of Badgley Court. A bright sunny morning,
  several days later. Enter LORD CLAVERTON *and*
  MONICA.

MONICA

Well, so far, it's better than you expected,
Isn't it, Father? They've let us alone;
The people in the dining room show no curiosity;
The beds are comfortable, the hot water is hot,
They give us a very tolerable breakfast;
And the chambermaid really *is* a chambermaid:
For when I asked about morning coffee
She said "I'm not the one for elevens's,
That's Nurse's business."

LORD CLAVERTON

                    So far, so good.
I'll feel more confidence after a fortnight—
After fourteen days of people not staring
Or offering picture papers, or wanting a fourth at bridge;
Still, I'll admit to a feeling of contentment
Already. I only hope that it will last—

The sense of wellbeing! It's often with us
When we are young, but then it's not noticed;
And by the time one has grown to consciousness
It comes less often.

                I hope this benignant sunshine
And warmth will last for a few days more.
But this early summer, that's hardly seasonable,
Is so often a harbinger of frost on the fruit trees.

MONICA

Oh, let's make the most of this weather while it lasts.
I never remember you as other than occupied
With anxieties from which you were longing to escape;
Now I want to see you learning to enjoy yourself!

LORD CLAVERTON

Perhaps I've never really enjoyed living
As much as most people. At least, as they seem to do.
Without knowing that they enjoy it. Whereas I've often
    known
That I didn't enjoy it. Some dissatisfaction
With myself, I suspect, very deep within myself
Has impelled me all my life to find justification
Not so much to the world—first of all to myself.
What is this self inside us, this silent observer,
Severe and speechless critic, who can terrorise us
And urge us on to futile activity,
And in the end, judge us still more severely
For the errors into which his own reproaches drove us?

MONICA

You admit that at the moment you find life pleasant,
That it really does seem quiet here and restful.
Even the matron, though she looks rather dominating,
Has left us alone.

LORD CLAVERTON

                    Yes, but remember   .
What she said. She said: "I'm going to leave you alone!
You want perfect peace: that's what Badgley Court is
      for."
I thought that very ominous. When people talk like that
It indicates a latent desire to interfere
With the privacy of others, which is certain to explode.

MONICA

Hush, Father. I see her coming from the house.
Take your newspaper and start reading to me.
[*Enter* MRS. PIGGOTT]

MRS. PIGGOTT

Good morning, Lord Claverton! Good morning, Miss
      Claverton!
Isn't this a glorious morning!
I'm afraid you'll think I've been neglecting you;
So I've come to apologise and explain.
I've been in such a rush, these last few days,
And I thought, "Lord Claverton will understand
My not coming in directly after breakfast:

He's led a busy life, too." But I hope you're happy?
Is there anything you need that hasn't been provided?
All you have to do is to make your wants known.
Just ring through to my office. If I'm not there
My secretary will be—Miss Timmins.
She'd be overjoyed to have the privilege of helping you!

MONICA

You're very kind . . . Oh, I'm sorry,
We don't know how we ought to address you.
Do we call you "Matron"?

MRS. PIGGOTT

                    Oh no, not "Matron"!
Of course, I *am* a matron in a sense—
No, I don't simply mean that I'm a married woman—
A widow in fact. But I was a Trained Nurse,
And of course I've always lived in what you might call
A medical milieu. My father was a specialist
In pharmacology. And my husband
Was a distinguished surgeon. Do you know, I fell in love
     with him
During an appendicitis operation!
I was a theatre nurse. But you mustn't call me "Matron"
At Badgley Court. You see, we've studied to avoid
Anything like a nursing-home atmosphere.
We don't want our guests to think of themselves as ill,
Though we never have guests who are perfectly well—
Except when they come like you, Miss Claverton.

MONICA

Claverton-Ferry. Or Ferry: it's shorter.

MRS. PIGGOTT

So sorry. Miss Claverton-Ferry. I'm Mrs. Piggott.
Just call me Mrs. Piggott. It's a short and simple name
And easy to remember. But, as I was saying,
Guests in perfect health are exceptional
Though we never accept any guest who's incurable.
You know, we've been deluged with applications
From people who wanted to come here to die!
We never accept them. Nor do we accept
Any guest who *looks* incurable—
We make that stipulation to all the doctors
Who send people here. When you go in to lunch
Just take a glance around the diningroom:
Nobody looks ill! They're all convalescents,
Or resting, like you. So you'll remember
Always to call me Mrs. Piggott, won't you?

MONICA

Yes, Mrs. Piggott, but please tell me one thing.
We haven't seen her yet, but the chambermaid
Referred to a nurse. When we see her
Do we address her as "Nurse"?

MRS. PIGGOTT

                    Oh yes, that's different.
She is a real nurse, you know, fully qualified.
Our system is very delicately balanced:

57

For me to be simply "Mrs. Piggott"
Reassures the guests in one respect;
And calling our nurses "Nurse" reassures them
In another respect.

LORD CLAVERTON

I follow you perfectly.

MRS. PIGGOTT

And now I must fly. I've so much on my hands!
But before I go, just let me tuck you up . . .
You must be very careful at this time of year;
This early warm weather can be very treacherous.
There, now you look more comfy. Don't let him stay out
    late
In the afternoon, Miss Claverton-Ferry.
And remember, when you want to be *very* quiet
There's the Silence Room. With a television set.
It's popular in the evenings. But not *too* crowded.

[Exit]

LORD CLAVERTON

Much as I had feared. But I'm not going to say
Nothing could be worse. Where there's a Mrs. Piggott
There may be, among the guests, something worse than
    Mrs. Piggott.

MONICA

Let's hope this was merely the concoction
Which she decants for every newcomer.

58

Perhaps after what she considers proper courtesies,
She will leave us alone.

[*Re-enter* MRS. PIGGOTT]

MRS. PIGGOTT

I really *am* neglectful!
Miss Claverton-Ferry, I ought to tell you more
About the amenities which Badgley Court
Can offer to guests of the younger generation.
When there are enough young people among us
We dance in the evening. At the moment there's no
    dancing,
And it's still too early for the bathing pool.
But several of our guests are keen on tennis,
And of course there's always croquet. But I don't advise
    croquet
Until you know enough about the other guests
To know whom *not* to play with. I'll mention no names,
But there are one or two who don't like being beaten,
And that spoils any sport, in my opinion.

MONICA

Thank you, Mrs. Piggott. But I'm very fond of walking
And I'm told there are very good walks in this neighbor-
    hood.

MRS. PIGGOTT

There are indeed. I can lend you a map.
There are lovely walks, on the shore or in the hills,
Quite away from the motor roads. You must learn the
    best walks.

I won't apologise for the lack of excitement:
After all, peace and quiet is our *raison d'être*.
Now I'll leave you to enjoy it.

[*Exit*]

MONICA

I hope she won't remember anything else.

LORD CLAVERTON

She'll come back to tell us more about the peace and
    quiet.

MONICA

I don't believe she'll be bothering us again:
I could see from her expression when she left
That she thought she'd done her duty by us for to-day.
I'm going to prowl about the grounds. Don't look so
    alarmed!
If you spy any guest who seems to be stalking you
Put your newspaper over your face
And pretend you're pretending to be asleep.
If they think you *are* asleep they'll do something to wake
    you,
But if they see you're shamming they'll have to take the
    hint.

[*Exit*]

A moment later, LORD CLAVERTON *spreads his newspaper
over his face. Enter* MRS. CARGHILL. *She sits in a
deckchair nearby, composes herself and takes out
her knitting.*

60

MRS. CARGHILL

[*after a pause*]

I hope I'm not disturbing you. I always sit here.
It's the sunniest and most sheltered corner,
And none of the other guests have discovered it.
It was clever of you to find it so quickly.
What made you choose it?

LORD CLAVERTON

[*throwing down newspaper*]

My daughter chose it.

She noticed that it seemed to offer the advantages
Which you have just mentioned. I am glad you can
    confirm them.

MRS. CARGHILL

Oh, so that *is* your daughter—that very charming girl?
And obviously devoted to her father.
I was watching you both in the diningroom last night.
You are the great Lord Claverton, aren't you?
Somebody said you were coming here—
It's been the topic of conversation.
But I couldn't believe that it would really happen!
And now I'm sitting here talking to you.
Dear me, it's astonishing, after all these years;
And you don't even recognize me! I'd know you any-
    where.
But then, we've all seen your portrait in the papers
So often. And everybody knows *you*. But still,
I wish you could have paid *me* that compliment,
    Richard.

61

Lord Claverton

What!

Mrs. Carghill

Don't you know me yet?

Lord Claverton

I'm afraid not.

Mrs. Carghill

There were the three of us—Effie, Maudie and me.
That day we spent on the river—I've never forgotten it—
The turning point of all my life!
Now whatever were the names of those friends of yours
And which one was it invited us to lunch?
I declare, I've utterly forgotten their names.
And you gave us lunch—I've forgotten what hotel—
But such a good lunch—and we all went in a punt
On the river—and we had a tea basket
With some lovely little cakes—I've forgotten what you
    called them,
And you made me try to punt, and I got soaking wet
And nearly dropped the punt pole, and you all laughed
    at me.
Don't you remember?

Lord Claverton

Pray continue.
The more you remind me of, the better I'll remember.

MRS. CARGHILL

And the three of us talked you over afterwards—
Effie and Maud and I. What a time ago it seems!
It's surprising I remember it all so clearly.
You attracted me, you know, at the very first meeting—
I can't think why, but it's the way things happen.
I said "there's a man I could follow round the world!"
But Effie it was—you know, Effie was very shrewd—
Effie it was said "you'd be throwing yourself away.
Mark my words" Effie said, "if you chose to follow *that*
        man
He'd give you the slip: he's not to be trusted.
That man is hollow." That's what she said.
Or did she say "yellow"? I'm not quite sure.
You do remember now, don't you, Richard?

LORD CLAVERTON

Not the conversation you have just repeated.
That is new to me. But I do remember you.

MRS. CARGHILL

Time has wrought sad changes in me, Richard.
I was very lovely once. So *you* thought,
And others thought so too. But as you remember,
Please, Richard, just repeat my name—just once:
The name by which you knew me. It would give me such
        a thrill
To hear you speak my name once more.

LORD CLAVERTON

Your name was Maisie Batterson.

MRS. CARGHILL

Oh, Richard, you're only saying that to tease me.
You know I meant my stage name. The name by which
you knew me.

LORD CLAVERTON

Well, then, Maisie Montjoy.

MRS. CARGHILL

Yes. Maisie Montjoy.
I was Maisie Montjoy once. And you didn't recognise
me.

LORD CLAVERTON

You've changed your name, no doubt. And I've changed
mine.
Your name now and here . . .

MRS. CARGHILL

Is Mrs. John Carghill.

LORD CLAVERTON

You married, I suppose, many years ago?

MRS. CARGHILL

Many years ago, the first time. That didn't last long.
People sometimes say: "Make one mistake in love,
You're more than likely to make another."

How true that is! Algy was a weakling,
But simple he was—not sly and slippery.
Then I married Mr. Carghill. Twenty years older
Than me, he was. Just what I needed.

LORD CLAVERTON

Is he still living?

MRS. CARGHILL

He had a weak heart.
And he worked too hard. Have you never heard
Of Carghill Equipments? They make office furniture.

LORD CLAVERTON

I've never had to deal with questions of equipment.
I trust that the business was very successful . . .
I mean, that he left you comfortably provided for?

MRS. CARGHILL

Well, Richard, my doctor could hardly have sent me
here
If I wasn't well off. Yes, I'm provided for.
But isn't it strange that you and I
Should meet here at last? Here, of all places!

LORD CLAVERTON

Why not, of all places? What I don't understand
Is why you should take the first opportunity,
Finding me here, to revive old memories
Which I should have thought we both preferred to leave
buried.

Mrs. Carghill

There you're wrong, Richard. Effie always said—
What a clever girl she was!—"he doesn't understand
      women.
Any woman who trusted *him* would soon find that out."
A man may prefer to forget all the women
He has loved. But a woman doesn't want to forget
A single one of her admirers. Why, even a faithless lover
Is still, in her memory, a kind of testimonial.
Men live by forgetting—women live on memories.
Besides a woman has nothing to be ashamed of:
A man is always trying to forget
His own shabby behaviour.

Lord Claverton

                    But we'd settled our account.
What harm was done? I learned my lesson
And you learned yours, if you needed the lesson.

Mrs. Carghill

You refuse to believe that I was really in love with you!
Well, it's natural that you shouldn't want to believe it.
But you think, or try to think, that if I'd really suffered
I shouldn't want to let you know who I am,
I shouldn't want to come and talk about the past.
You're wrong, you know. It's both pain and pleasure
To talk about the past—about you and me.
These memories are painful—but I cherish them.

LORD CLAVERTON

If you had really been broken-hearted
I can't see how you could have acted as you did.

MRS. CARGHILL

Who can say whether a heart's been broken
Once it's been repaired? But I know what you mean.
You mean that I would never have started an action
For breach of promise, if I'd really cared for you.
What sentimental nonsense! One starts an action
Simply because one must do *something*.
Well, perhaps I shouldn't have settled out of court.
My lawyer said: "I advise you to accept,
Because Mr. Ferry will be standing for Parliament:
His father has political ambitions for him.
If he's lost a breach of promise suit
Some people won't want to appear as his supporters."
He said: "What his lawyers are offering in settlement
Is twice as much as I think you'd be awarded."
Effie was against it—she wanted you exposed.
But I gave way. I didn't want to ruin you.
If I'd carried on, it might have ended your career,
And then you wouldn't have become Lord Claverton.
So perhaps I laid the foundation of your fortunes!

LORD CLAVERTON

And perhaps at the same time of your own?
I seem to remember, it was only a year or so
Before your name appeared in very large letters
In Shaftesbury Avenue.

MRS. CARGHILL

Yes, I had my art.
Don't you remember what a hit I made
With a number called *It's Not Too Late For You To
Love Me?*
I couldn't have put the feeling into it I did
But for what I'd gone through. Did you hear me sing it?

LORD CLAVERTON

Yes, I heard you sing it.

MRS. CARGHILL

And what did you feel?

LORD CLAVERTON

Nothing at all. I remember my surprise
At finding that I felt nothing at all.
I thought, perhaps, what a lucky escape
It had been, for both of us.

MRS. CARGHILL

That "both of us"
Was an afterthought, Richard. A lucky escape
You thought, for you. You felt no embarrassment?

LORD CLAVERTON

Why should I feel embarrassment? My conscience was
clear.
A brief infatuation, ended in the only way possible
To our mutual satisfaction.

Mrs. Carghill

                         Your conscience was clear.
I've very seldom heard people mention their consciences
Except to observe that their consciences were clear.
You got out of a tangle for a large cash payment
And no publicity. So your conscience was clear.
At bottom, I believe you're still the same silly Richard
You always were. You wanted to pose
As a man of the world. And now you're posing
As what? I presume, as an elder statesman;
And the difference between being an elder statesman
And posing successfully as an elder statesman
Is practically negligible. And you look the part.
Whatever part you've played, I must say you've always
        looked it.

Lord Claverton

I've no longer any part to play, Maisie.

Mrs. Carghill

There'll always be some sort of part for you
Right to the end. You'll still be playing a part
In your obituary, whoever writes it.

Lord Claverton

Considering how long ago it was when you knew me
And considering the brevity of our acquaintance,
You're surprisingly confident, I must say,
About your understanding of my character.

I've followed your progress year by year, Richard.
And although it's true that our acquaintance was brief,
Our relations were intense enough, I think,
To have given me one or two insights into you.
No, Richard, don't imagine that I'm still in love with
    you;
And you needn't think I idolise your memory.
It's simply that I feel that we belong together . . .
Now, don't get alarmed. But you touched my soul—
Pawed it, perhaps, and the touch still lingers.
And I've touched yours.
It's frightening to think that we're still together
And more frightening to think that we may *always* be
    together.
There's a phrase I seem to remember reading some-
    where:
Where their fires are not quenched. Do you know what
    I do?
I read your letters every night.

Lord Claverton

My letters!

Mrs. Carghill

Have you forgotten that you wrote me letters?
Oh, not very many. Only a few worth keeping.
Only a few. But very beautiful!
It was Effie said, when the break came,

70

"They'll be worth a fortune to you, Maisie."
They would have figured at the trial, I suppose,
If there had been a trial. Don't you remember them?

LORD CLAVERTON

Vaguely. Were they very passionate?

MRS. CARGHILL

They were very loving. Would you like to read them?
I'm afraid I can't show you the originals;
They're in my lawyer's safe. But I have photostats
Which are quite as good, I'm told. And I like to read
     them
In your own handwriting.

LORD CLAVERTON

                        And have you shown these letters
To many people?

MRS. CARGHILL

                 Only a few friends.
Effie said: "If he becomes a famous man
And you should be in want, you could have these letters
     auctioned."
Yes, I'll bring the photostats tomorrow morning,
And read them to you.
                     —Oh, there's Mrs. Piggott!
She's bearing down on us. Isn't she frightful!
She never stops talking. Can you bear it?

71

If I go at once, perhaps she'll take the hint
And leave us alone tomorrow.

                              Good morning, Mrs. Piggott!
Isn't it a glorious morning!
[*Enter* Mrs. Piggott]

Mrs. Piggott

Good morning, Mrs. Carghill!

Mrs. Carghill

                              Dear Mrs. Piggott!
It seems to me that you never sit still:
You simply sacrifice yourself for us.

Mrs. Piggott

It's the breath of life to me, Mrs. Carghill,
Attending to my guests. I like to feel they *need* me!

Mrs. Carghill

You do look after us well, Mrs. Piggott:
You're so considerate—and so understanding.

Mrs. Piggott

But I ought to introduce you. You've been talking to
    Lord Claverton,
The famous Lord Claverton. This is Mrs. Carghill.
Two of our very nicest guests!
I just came to see that Lord Claverton was comfortable:
We can't allow him to tire himself with talking.
What he needs is *rest!* You're not going, Mrs. Carghill?

72

MRS. CARGHILL

Oh, I knew that Lord Claverton had come for a rest cure,
And it struck me that he might find it a strain
To have to cope with both of us at once.
Besides, I ought to do my breathing exercises.

[*Exit*]

MRS. PIGGOTT

As a matter of fact, I flew to your rescue
(That's why I've brought your morning tipple myself
Instead of leaving it, as usual, to Nurse)
When I saw that Mrs. Carghill had caught you.
You wouldn't know that name, but you might remem-
    ber her
As Maisie Montjoy in revue.
She was well-known at one time. I'm afraid her name
Means nothing at all to the younger generation,
But you and I should remember her, Lord Claverton.
That tune she was humming, *It's Not Too Late For You
    To Love Me*,
Everybody was singing it once. A charming person,
I dare say, but not quite your sort or mine.
I suspected that she wanted to meet you, so I thought
That I'd take the first opportunity of hinting—
Tactfully, of course—that you should not be disturbed.
Well, she's gone now. If she bothers you again
Just let me know. I'm afraid it's the penalty
Of being famous.
[*Enter* MONICA]

73

Oh, Miss Claverton-Ferry!
I didn't see you coming. Now I must fly.

[*Exit*]

MONICA

I saw Mrs. Piggott bothering you again
So I hurried to your rescue. You look tired, Father.
She ought to know better. But I'm all the more distressed
Because I have some . . . not very good news for you.

LORD CLAVERTON

Oh, indeed. What's the matter?

MONICA

I didn't get far.
I met Michael in the drive. He says he must see you.
I'm afraid that something unpleasant has happened.

LORD CLAVERTON

Was he driving his car?

MONICA

No, he was walking.

LORD CLAVERTON

I hope he's not had another accident.
You know, after that last escapade of his,
I've lived in terror of his running over somebody.

74

MONICA

Why, Father, should you be afraid of that?
This shows how bad your nerves have been.
He only ran into a tree.

LORD CLAVERTON

Yes, a tree.
It might have been a man. But it can't be that,
Or he wouldn't be at large. Perhaps he's in trouble
With some woman or other. I'm sure he has friends
Whom he wouldn't care for you or me to know about.

MONICA

It's probably money.

LORD CLAVERTON

If it's only debts
Once more, I expect I can put up with it.
But where is he?

MONICA

I told him he must wait in the garden
Until I have prepared you. I've made him understand
That the doctors want you to be free from worry.
He won't make a scene. But I can see he's frightened.
And you know what Michael is like when he's
     frightened.
He's apt to be sullen and quick to take offence.
So I hope you'll be patient.

LORD CLAVERTON

Well then, fetch him.
Let's get this over.

MONICA

[*calls*] Michael!
[*Enter* MICHAEL]

LORD CLAVERTON

Good morning, Michael.

MICHAEL

Good morning, Father.
[*A pause*]
What a lovely day!
I'm glad you're here, to enjoy such weather.

LORD CLAVERTON

You're glad I'm here? Did you drive down from London?

MICHAEL

I drove down last night. I'm staying at a pub
About two miles from here. Not a bad little place.

LORD CLAVERTON

Why are you staying there? I shouldn't have thought
It would be the sort of place that you'd choose for a
    holiday.

76

MICHAEL

Well, this isn't a holiday exactly.
But this hotel was very well recommended.
Good cooking, for a country inn. And not at all expen-
sive.

LORD CLAVERTON

You don't normally consider that a recommendation.
Are you staying there long? For the whole of this
holiday?

MICHAEL

Well, this isn't a holiday, exactly.
Oh. I said that before, didn't I?

MONICA

I wish you'd stop being so polite to each other.
Michael, you know what you've come to ask of Father
And Father knows that you want something from him.
Perhaps you'll get to the point if I leave you together.

[*Exit*]

MICHAEL

You know, it's awfully hard to explain things to *you*.
You've always made up your mind that I was to blame
Before you knew the facts. The first thing I remember
Is being blamed for something I hadn't done.
I never got over that. If you always blame a person
It's natural he should end by getting into trouble.

77

LORD CLAVERTON

You started pretty early getting into trouble,
When you were expelled from your prep school for
    stealing.
But come to the point. You're in trouble again.
We'll ignore, if you please, the question of blame:
Which will spare you the necessity of blaming someone
    else.
Just tell me what's happened.

MICHAEL

Well, I've lost my job.

LORD CLAVERTON

The position that Sir Alfred Walter made for you.

MICHAEL

I'd stuck it for two years. And deadly dull it was.

LORD CLAVERTON

Every job is dull, nine-tenths of the time . . .

MICHAEL

I need something much more stimulating.

LORD CLAVERTON

Well?

MICHAEL

I want to find some more speculative business.

78

LORD CLAVERTON

I dare say you've tried a little private speculation.

MICHAEL

Several of my friends gave me excellent tips.
They always came off—the tips I didn't take.

LORD CLAVERTON

And the ones you did take?

MICHAEL

                    Not so well, for some reason.
The fact is, I needed a good deal more capital
To make anything of it. If I could have borrowed more
I might have pulled it off.

LORD CLAVERTON

                    Borrowed? From whom?
Not . . . from the firm?

MICHAEL

                    I went to a lender,
A man whom a friend of mine recommended.
He gave me good terms, on the strength of my name:
The only good the name has ever done me.

LORD CLAVERTON

On the strength of your name. And what do you call
    good terms?

MICHAEL

I'd nothing at all to pay for two years:
The interest was just added on to the capital.

LORD CLAVERTON

And how long ago was that?

MICHAEL

Nearly two years.
Time passes pretty quickly, when you're in debt.

LORD CLAVERTON

And have you other debts?

MICHAEL

Oh, ordinary debts:
My tailor's bill, for instance.

LORD CLAVERTON

I expected that.
It was just the same at Oxford.

MICHAEL

It's their own fault.
They won't send in their bills, and then I forget them.
It's being your son that gets me into debt.
Just because of your name they insist on giving credit.

LORD CLAVERTON

And your debts: are they the cause of your being discharged?

80

MICHAEL

Well, partly. Sir Alfred did come to hear about it,
And so he pretended to be very shocked.
Said he couldn't retain any man on his staff
Who'd taken to gambling. Called me a gambler!
Said he'd communicate with you about it.

LORD CLAVERTON

That accounts for your coming down here so precipi-
   tately—
In order to let me have your version first.
I dare say Sir Alfred's will be rather different.
And what else did he say?

MICHAEL

                    He took the usual line,
Just like the headmaster. And my tutor at Oxford.
"Not what we expected from the son of your father"
And that sort of thing. It's for your sake, he says,
That he wants to keep things quiet. I can tell you, it's
   no joke
Being the son of a famous public man.
You don't know what I suffered, working in that office.
In the first place, they all knew the job had been made
   for me
Because I was your son. They considered me superfluous;
They knew I couldn't be living on my pay;
They had a lot of fun with me—sometimes they'd
   pretend

That I was overworked, when I'd nothing to do.
Even the office boys began to sneer at me.
I wonder I stood it as long as I did.

LORD CLAVERTON

And does this bring us to the end of the list of your
  shortcomings?
Or did Sir Alfred make other unflattering criticisms?

MICHAEL

Well, there was one thing he brought up against me,
That I'd been too familiar with one of the girls.
He assumed it had gone a good deal further than it had.

LORD CLAVERTON

Perhaps it had gone further than you're willing to
  admit.

MICHAEL

Well, after all, she was the only one
Who was at all nice to me. She wasn't exciting,
But it served to pass the time. It would never have
  happened
If only I'd been given some interesting work!

LORD CLAVERTON

And what do you now propose to do with yourself?

MICHAEL

I want to go abroad.

LORD CLAVERTON

You want to go abroad?
Well, that's not a bad idea. A few years out of England
In one of the Dominions, might set you on your feet.
I have connections, or at least correspondents
Almost everywhere. Australia—no.
The men I know there are all in the cities:
An outdoor life would suit you better.
How would you like to go to Western Canada?
Or what about sheep farming in New Zealand?

MICHAEL

Sheep farming? Good Lord, no.
That's not my idea. I want to make money.
I want to be somebody on my own account.

LORD CLAVERTON

But what do you want to do? Where do you want to go?
What kind of a life do you think you want?

MICHAEL

I simply want to lead a life of my own,
According to my own ideas of good and bad,
Of right and wrong. I want to go far away
To some country where no one has heard the name of
        Claverton;
Or where, if I took a different name—and I might choose
        to—
No one would know or care what my name had been.

LORD CLAVERTON

So you are ready to repudiate your family,
To throw away the whole of your inheritance?

MICHAEL

What is my inheritance? As for your title,
I know why you took it. And Mother knew.
First, because it gave you the opportunity
Of retiring from politics, not without dignity,
Being no longer wanted. And you wished to be Lord
    Claverton
Also, to hold your own with Mother's family—
To lord it over them, in fact. Oh, I've no doubt
That the thought of passing on your name and title
To a son, was gratifying. But it wasn't for *my* sake!
I was just *your* son—that is to say,
A kind of prolongation of your existence,
A representative carrying on business in your absence.
Why should I thank you for imposing this upon me?
And what satisfaction, I wonder, will it give you
In the grave? If you're still conscious after death,
I bet it will be a surprised state of consciousness.
Poor ghost! reckoning up its profit and loss
And wondering why it bothered about such trifles.

LORD CLAVERTON

So you want me to help you to escape from your father!

MICHAEL

And to help my father to be rid of *me*.
You simply don't know how very much pleasanter

84

You will find life become, once I'm out of the country.
What I'd like is a chance to go abroad
As a partner in some interesting business.
But I might be expected to put up some capital.

LORD CLAVERTON

What sort of business have you in mind?

MICHAEL

Oh, I don't know. Import and export,
With an opportunity of profits both ways.

LORD CLAVERTON

This is what I will do for you, Michael.
I will help you to make a start in any business
You may find for yourself—if, on investigation,
I am satisfied about the nature of the business.

MICHAEL

Anyway, I'm determined to get out of England.

LORD CLAVERTON

Michael! Are there reasons for your wanting to go
Beyond what you've told me? It isn't . . . manslaughter?

MICHAEL

Manslaughter? Why manslaughter? Oh, you mean on
the road.
Certainly not. I'm far too good a driver.

LORD CLAVERTON

What then? That young woman?

MICHAEL

                     I'm not such a fool
As to get myself involved in a breach of promise suit
Or somebody's divorce. No, you needn't worry
About that girl—or any other.
But I want to get out. I'm fed up with England.

LORD CLAVERTON

I'm sure you don't mean that. But it's natural enough
To want a few years abroad. It might be very good for
     you
To find your feet. But I shouldn't like to think
That what inspired you was no positive ambition
But only the desire to escape.

MICHAEL

                I'm not a fugitive.

LORD CLAVERTON

No, not a fugitive from justice—
Only a fugitive from reality.
Oh Michael! If you had some aim of high achievement,
Some dream of excellence, how gladly would I help you!
Even though it carried you away from me forever
To suffer the monotonous sun of the tropics
Or shiver in the northern night. Believe me, Michael:
Those who flee from their past will always lose the race.

I know this from experience. When you reach your goal,
Your imagined paradise of success and grandeur,
You will find your past failures waiting there to greet
    you.
You're all I have to live for, Michael—
You and Monica. If I lived for twenty years
Knowing that my son had played the coward—
I should merely be another twenty years in dying.

MICHAEL

Very well: if you like, call me a coward.
I wonder whether you would play the hero
If you were in my place. I don't believe you would.
You didn't suffer from the handicap that I've had.
Your father was rich, but was no one in particular,
So you'd nothing to live up to. Those standards of con-
    duct
You've always made so much of, for my benefit:
I wonder whether *you* have always lived up to them.
       [MONICA *has entered unobserved*]

MONICA

Michael! How can you speak to Father like that?
Father! What has happened? Why do you look so angry?
I know that Michael must be in great trouble,
So can't you help him?

LORD CLAVERTON

         I am trying to help him,
And to meet him half way. I have made him an offer

87

Which he must think over. But if he goes abroad
I want him to go in a very different spirit
From that which he has just been exhibiting.

MONICA

Michael! Say something.

MICHAEL

What is there to say?
I want to leave England, and make my own career:
And Father simply calls me a coward.

MONICA

Father! You know that I would give my life for you.
Oh, how silly that phrase sounds! But there's no vocabu-
lary
For love within a family, love that's lived in
But not looked at, love within the light of which
All else is seen, the love within which
All other love finds speech.
This love is silent.
What can I say to you?
However Michael has behaved, Father,
Whatever Father has said, Michael,
You must forgive each other, you must love each other.

MICHAEL

I could have loved Father, if he'd wanted love,
But he never did, Monica, not from me.
You know I've always been very fond of you—

I've a very affectionate nature, really,
But . . .

[*Enter* MRS. CARGHILL *with despatch-case*]

MRS. CARGHILL

Richard! I didn't think you'd still be here.
I came back to have a quiet read of your letters;
But how nice to find a little family party!
I know who you are! You're Monica, of course:
And this must be your brother, Michael.
I'm right, aren't I?

MICHAEL
                    Yes, you're right.
But . . .

MRS. CARGHILL
        How did I know? Because you're so like your father
When he was your age. He's the picture of you, Richard,
As you were once. You're not to introduce us,
I'll introduce myself. I'm Maisie Montjoy!
That means nothing to you, my dears.
It's a very long time since the name of Maisie Montjoy
Topped the bill in revue. Now I'm Mrs. John Carghill.
Richard! It's astonishing about your children:
Monica hardly resembles you at all,
But Michael—your father has changed a good deal
Since I knew him ever so many years ago,
Yet you're the image of what he was then.
Your father was a very dear friend of mine once.

89

MICHAEL

Did he really look like me?

MRS. CARGHILL

You've his voice! and his way of moving! It's marvellous.
And the charm! He's inherited all of your charm, Rich-
ard.
There's no denying it. But who's this coming?
It's another new guest here. He's waving to us.
Do you know him, Richard?

LORD CLAVERTON

It's a man I used to know.

MRS. CARGHILL

How interesting! He's a very good figure
And he's rather exotic-looking. Is he a foreigner?

LORD CLAVERTON

He comes from some place in Central America.

MRS. CARGHILL

How romantic! I'd love to meet him.
He's coming to speak to us. You must introduce him.
[*Enter* GOMEZ]

GOMEZ

Good morning, Dick.

LORD CLAVERTON

Good morning, Fred.

90

GOMEZ

You weren't expecting me to join you here, were you?
You're here for a rest cure. I persuaded my doctor
That I was in need of a rest cure too.
And when I heard you'd chosen to come to Badgley
    Court
I said to my doctor, "Well, what about it?
What better recommendation could I have?"
So he sent me here.

MRS. CARGHILL

                    Oh, you've seen each other lately?
Richard, I think that you might introduce us.

LORD CLAVERTON

Oh. This is . . .

GOMEZ

                    Your old friend Federico Gomez,
The prominent citizen of San Marco.
That's my name.

LORD CLAVERTON

                    So let me introduce you—by that name—
To Mrs. . . . Mrs. . . .

MRS. CARGHILL

                    Mrs. John Carghill.

GOMEZ

We seem a bit weak on the surnames, Dick!

91

MRS. CARGHILL

Well, you see, Señor Gomez, when we first became
    friends—
Lord Claverton and I—I was known by my stage name.
There was a time, once, when everyone in London
Knew the name of Maisie Montjoy in revue.

GOMEZ

If Maisie Montjoy was as beautiful to look at
As Mrs. Carghill, I can well understand
Her success on the stage.

MRS. CARGHILL

              Oh, did you never see me?
That's a pity, Señor Gomez.

GOMEZ

              I lost touch with things in England.
Had I been in London, and in Dick's position
I should have been your most devoted admirer.

MRS. CARGHILL

It's Not Too Late For You To Love Me! That's the
    song
That made my reputation, Señor Gomez.

GOMEZ

It will never be too late. Don't you agree, Dick?
—This young lady I take to be your daughter?
And this is your son?

LORD CLAVERTON

      This is my son Michael,
And my daughter Monica.

MONICA

      How do you do.

Michael!

MICHAEL

   How do you do.

MRS. CARGHILL

I don't believe you've known Lord Claverton
As long as I have, Señor Gomez.

GOMEZ

My dear lady, you're not old enough
To have known Dick Ferry as long as I have.
We were friends at Oxford.

MRS. CARGHILL

      Oh, so you were at Oxford!
Is that how you come to speak such perfect English?
Of course, I could tell from your looks that you were
    Spanish.
I do like Spaniards. They're so aristocratic.
But it's very strange that we never met before.
You were a friend of Richard's at Oxford
And Richard and I became great friends
Not long afterwards, didn't we, Richard?

93

GOMEZ

I expect that was after I had left England.

MRS. CARGHILL

Of course, that explains it. After Oxford
I suppose you went back to . . . where is your home?

GOMEZ

The republic of San Marco.

MRS. CARGHILL

Went back to San Marco.
Señor Gomez, if it's true you're staying at Badgley Court,
I warn you—I'm going to cross-examine you
And make you tell me all about Richard
In his Oxford days.

GOMEZ

On one condition:
That you tell me all about Dick when you knew him.

MRS. CARGHILL

[pats her despatch-case]

Secret for secret, Señor Gomez!
You've got to be the first to put your cards on the table!

MONICA

Father, I think you should take your rest now.
—I must explain that the doctors were very insistent
That my father should rest and have absolute quiet
Before every meal.

94

LORD CLAVERTON

But Michael and I
Must continue our discussion. This afternoon, Michael.

MONICA

No, I think you've had enough talk for to-day.
Michael, as you're staying so close at hand
Will you come back in the morning? After breakfast?

LORD CLAVERTON

Yes, come tomorrow morning.

MICHAEL

Well, I'll come tomorow morning.

MRS. CARGHILL

Are you staying in the neighbourhood, Michael?
Your father is such an old friend of mine
That is seems most natural to call you Michael.
You don't mind, do you?

MICHAEL

No, I don't mind.
I'm staying at the George—it's not far away.

MRS. CARGHILL

Then I'd like to walk a little way with you.

MICHAEL

Delighted, I'm sure.

95

GOMEZ

Taking a holiday?
You're in business in London, aren't you?

MICHAEL

Not a holiday, no. I've been in business in London,
But I think of cutting loose, and going abroad.

MRS. CARGHILL

You must tell me all about it. Perhaps I could advise
    you.
We'll leave you now, Richard. Au revoir, Monica.
And Señor Gomez, I shall hold you to your promise!
                    [*Exeunt* MRS. CARGHILL *and* MICHAEL]

GOMEZ

Well, Dick, we've got to obey our doctors' orders.
But while we're here, we must have some good talks
About old times. Bye bye for the present.
                                            [*Exit*]

MONICA

Father, those awful people. We mustn't stay here.
I want you to escape from them.

LORD CLAVERTON

                        What I want to escape from
Is myself, is the past. But what a coward I am,
To talk of escaping! And what a hypocrite!
A few minutes ago I was pleading with Michael

96

Not to try to escape from his own past failures:
I said I knew from experience. Do I understand the
 meaning
Of the lesson I would teach? Come, I'll start to learn
 again.
Michael and I shall go to school together.
We'll sit side by side, at little desks
And suffer the same humiliations
At the hands of the same master. But have I still time?
There is time for Michael. Is it too late for me, Monica?

CURTAIN

Act Three

Same as Act Two. Late afternoon of the following day.
Monica *seated alone. Enter* Charles.

Charles

Well, Monica, here I am. I hope you got my message.

Monica

Oh Charles, Charles, Charles, I'm so glad you've come!
I've been so worried, and rather frightened.
It was exasperating that they couldn't find me
When you telephoned this morning. That Mrs. Piggott
Should have heard my beloved's voice
And I couldn't, just when I had been yearning
For the sound of it, for the caress that is in it!
Oh Charles, how I've wanted you! And now I *need* you.

Charles

My darling, what I want is to know that you need me.
On that last day in London, you admitted that you loved
    me,
But I wondered . . . I'm sorry, I couldn't help wonder-
    ing

How much your words meant. You didn't seem to need
    me then.
And you said we weren't engaged yet . . .

MONICA

               We're engaged now.
At least *I'm* engaged. I'm engaged to you for ever.

CHARLES

There's another shopping expedition we must make!
But my darling, since I got your letter this morning
About your father and Michael, and those people from
    his past,
I've been trying to think what I could do to help him.
If it's blackmail, and that's very much what it looks like,
Do you think I could persuade him to confide in me?

MONICA

Oh Charles! How could anyone blackmail Father?
Father, of all people the most scrupulous,
The most austere. It's quite impossible.
Father with a guilty secret in his past!
I just can't imagine it.
    [CLAVERTON *has entered unobserved*]

MONICA

I never expected you from *that* direction, Father!
I thought you were indoors. Where have you been?

LORD CLAVERTON

Not far away. Standing under the great beech tree.

100

MONICA

Why under the beech tree?

LORD CLAVERTON

I feel drawn to that spot.
No matter. I heard what you said about guilty secrets.
There are many things not crimes, Monica,
Beyond anything of which the law takes cognisance:
Temporary failures, irreflective aberrations,
Reckless surrenders, unexplainable impulses,
Moments we regret in the very next moment,
Episodes we try to conceal from the world.
Has there been nothing in your life, Charles Hemington,
Which you wish to forget? Which you wish to keep un-
   known?

CHARLES

There are certainly things I would gladly forget, Sir,
Or rather, which I wish had never happened.
I can think of things you don't yet know about me,
   Monica,
But there's nothing I would ever wish to conceal from
   you.

LORD CLAVERTON

If there's nothing, truly nothing, that you couldn't tell
   Monica
Then all is well with you. You're in love with each
   other—
I don't need to be told what I've seen for myself!

And if there is nothing that you conceal from *her*
However important you may consider it
To conceal from the rest of the world—your soul is safe.
If a man has one person, just one in his life,
To whom he is willing to confess everything—
And that includes, mind you, not only things criminal,
Not only turpitude, meanness and cowardice,
But also situations which are simply ridiculous,
When he has played the fool (as who has not?)—
Then he loves that person, and his love will save him.
I'm afraid that I've never loved anyone, really.
No, I do love my Monica—but there's the impediment:
It's impossible to be quite honest with your child
If you've never been honest with anyone older,
On terms of equality. To one's child one can't reveal
    oneself
While she is a child. And by the time she's grown
You've woven such a web of fiction about you!
I've spent my life in trying to forget myself,
In trying to identify myself with the part
I had chosen to play. And the longer we pretend
The harder it becomes to drop the pretence,
Walk off the stage, change into our own clothes
And speak as ourselves. So I'd become an idol
To Monica. She worshipped the part I played:
How could I be sure that she would love the actor
If she saw him, off the stage, without his costume and
    makeup
And without his stage words. Monica!
I've had your love under false pretences.

Now, I'm tired of keeping up those pretences,
But I hope that you'll find a little love in your heart
Still, for your father, when you know him
For what he is, the broken-down actor.

MONICA

I think I should only love you the better, Father,
The more I knew about you. I should understand you
    better.
There's nothing I'm afraid of learning about Charles,
There's nothing I'm afraid of learning about you.

CHARLES

I was thinking, Sir—forgive the suspicion—
From what Monica has told me about your fellow guests,
Two persons who, she says, claim a very long acquaint-
    ance—
I was thinking that if there's any question of blackmail,
I've seen something of it in my practice at the bar.
I'm sure I could help.

MONICA

Oh Father, do let him.

CHARLES

At least, I think I know the best man to advise you.

LORD CLAVERTON

Blackmail? Yes, I've heard that word before,
Not so very long ago. When I asked him what he wanted.
Oh no, he said, I want nothing from you

Except your friendship and your company.
He's a very rich man. And she's a rich woman.
If people merely blackmail you to get your company
I'm afraid the law can't touch them.

CHARLES

Then why should you submit?
Why not leave Badgley and escape from them?

LORD CLAVERTON

Because they are not real, Charles. They are merely
    ghosts:
Spectres from my past. They've always been with me
Though it was not till lately that I found the living
    persons
Whose ghosts tormented me, to be only human beings,
Malicious, petty, and I see myself emerging
From my spectral existence into something like reality.

MONICA

But what did the ghosts mean? All these years
You've kept them to yourself. Did Mother know of
    them?

LORD CLAVERTON

Your mother knew nothing about them. And I know
That I never knew your mother, as she never knew me.
I thought that she would never understand
Or that she would be jealous of the ghosts who haunted
    me.

104

And I'm still of that opinion. How open one's heart
When one is sure of the wrong response?
How make a confession with no hope of absolution?
It was not her fault. We never understood each other.
And so we lived, with a deep silence between us,
And she died silently. She had nothing to say to me.
I think of your mother, when she lay dying:
Completely without interest in the life that lay behind
    her
And completely indifferent to whatever lay ahead of her.

MONICA

It is time to break the silence! Let us share your ghosts!

CHARLES

But these are only human beings, who can be dealt
    with.

MONICA

Or only ghosts, who can be exorcised!
Who are they, and what do they stand for in your life?

LORD CLAVERTON

. . . And yet they've both done better for themselves
In consequence of it all. He admitted as much,
Fred Culverwell . . .

MONICA

Fred Culverwell?
Who is Fred Culverwell?

LORD CLAVERTON

He no longer exists,

He's Federico Gomez, the Central American,

A man who's made a fortune by his own peculiar methods,

A man of great importance and the highest standing

In his adopted country. He even has sons

Following in their father's footsteps

Who are also successful. What would *he* have been

If he hadn't known me? Only a schoolmaster

In an obscure grammar school somewhere in the Midlands.

As for Maisie Batterson . . .

MONICA

Maisie Batterson?

Who is Maisie Batterson?

LORD CLAVERTON

She no longer exists.

Nor the musical comedy star, Maisie Montjoy.

There is Mrs. John Carghill, the wealthy widow.

But Freddy Culverwell and Maisie Batterson,

And Dick Ferry too, and Richard Ferry—

These are my ghosts. They were people with good in them,

People who might all have been very different

From Gomez, Mrs. Carghill and Lord Claverton.

Freddy admired me, when we were at Oxford:

106

What did I make of his admiration?
I led him to acquire tastes beyond his means:
So he became a forger. And so he served his term.
Was I responsible for that weakness in him?
Yes, I was.
How easily we ignore the fact that those who admire us
Will imitate our vices as well as our virtues—
Or whatever the qualities for which they did admire us!
And that again may nourish the faults that they were
        born with.
And Maisie loved me, with whatever capacity
For loving she had—self-centred and foolish—
But we should respect love always when we meet it;
Even when it's vain and selfish, we must not abuse it.
That is where I failed. And the memory frets me.

CHARLES

But all the same, these two people mustn't persecute you.
We can't allow that. What hold have they upon you?

LORD CLAVERTON

Only the hold of those who know
Something discreditable, dishonourable . . .

MONICA

Then, Father, you should tell *us* what they already know.
Why should you wish to conceal from those who love
        you
What is known so well to those who hate you?

                                 I will tell you very briefly
And simply. As for Frederick Culverwell,
He re-enters my life to make himself a reminder
Of one occasion the memory of which,
He knows very well, has always haunted me.
I was driving back to Oxford. We had two girls with us.
It was late at night. A secondary road.
I ran over an old man lying in the road
And I did not stop. Then another man ran over him.
A lorry driver. He stopped and was arrested,
But was later discharged. It was definitely shown
That the old man had died a natural death
And had been run over after he was dead.
It was only a corpse that we had run over
So neither of us killed him. But *I* didn't stop.
And all my life I have heard, from time to time,
When I least expected, between waking and sleeping,
A voice that whispered, "you didn't stop!"
I knew the voice: it was Fred Culverwell's.

MONICA

Poor Father! All your life! And no one to share it with;
I never knew how lonely you were
Or why you were lonely.

CHARLES

                And Mrs. Carghill:
What has she against you?

108

Lord Claverton

I was her first lover.
I would have married her—but my father prevented
    that:
Made it worth while for her not to marry me—
That was his way of putting it—and of course
Made it worth while for me not to marry her.
In fact, we were wholly unsuited to each other,
Yet she had a peculiar physical attraction
Which no other woman has had. And she knows it.
And she knows that the ghost of the man I was
Still clings to the ghost of the woman who was Maisie.
We should have been poor, we should certainly have
    quarrelled,
We should have been unhappy, might have come to
    divorce;
But she hasn't forgotten or forgiven me.

Charles

This man, and this woman, who are so vindictive:
Don't you see that they were as much at fault as you
And that they know it? That's why they are inspired
With revenge—it's their means of self-justification.
Let them tell their versions of their miserable stories,
Confide them in whispers. They cannot harm you.

Lord Claverton

Your reasoning's sound enough. But it's irrelevant.
Each of them remembers an occasion
On which I ran away. Very well.

109

I shan't run away now—run away from *them*.
It is through this meeting that I shall at last escape them.
—I've made my confession to you, Monica:
That is the first step taken towards my freedom,
And perhaps the most important. I know what you
    think.
You think that I suffer from a morbid conscience,
From brooding over faults I might well have forgotten.
You think that I'm sickening, when I'm just recovering!
It's hard to make other people realise
The magnitude of things that appear to them petty;
It's harder to confess the sin that no one believes in
Than the crime that everyone can appreciate.
For the crime is in relation to the law
And the sin is in relation to the sinner.
What has made the difference in the last five minutes
Is not the heinousness of my misdeeds
But the fact of my confession. And to you, Monica,
To you, of all people.

CHARLES

        I grant you all that.
But what do you propose? How long, Lord Claverton,
Will you stay here and endure this persecution?

LORD CLAVERTON

To the end. The place and time of liberation
Are, I think, determined. Let us say no more about it.
Meanwhile, I feel sure they are conspiring against me.
I see Mrs. Carghill coming.

MONICA

Let us go.

LORD CLAVERTON

We will stay here. Let her join us.
[*Enter* MRS. CARGHILL]

MRS. CARGHILL

I've been hunting high and low for you, Richard!
I've some very exciting news for you!
But I suspect . . . Dare I? Yes, I'm sure of it, Monica!
I can tell by the change in your expression to-day;
This must be your fiancé. Do introduce him.

MONICA

Mr. Charles Hemington. Mrs. Carghill.

CHARLES

How do you do.

MRS. CARGHILL

What a charming name!

CHARLES

I'm glad my name meets with your approval, Mrs.
Carghill.

MRS. CARGHILL

And let me congratulate *you,* Mr. Hemington.
You're a very lucky man, to get a girl like Monica.

111

I take a great interest in her future.
Fancy, I've only known her two days!
But I feel like a mother to her already.
You may say that I just missed being her mother!
I've known her father for a very long time,
And there was a moment when I almost married him,
Oh so long ago. So you see, Mr. Hemington,
I've come to regard her as my adopted daughter.
So much so, that it seems odd to call you Mr. Heming-
   ton:
I'm going to call you Charles!

CHARLES

As you please, Mrs. Carghill.

LORD CLAVERTON

You said you had some exciting news for us.
Would you care to impart it?

MRS. CARGHILL

                    It's about dear Michael.

LORD CLAVERTON

Oh? What about Michael?

MRS. CARGHILL

                    He's told me all his story.
You've cruelly misunderstood him, Richard.
How he must have suffered! So I put on my thinking
   cap.

112

I know you've always thought me utterly brainless,
But I have an idea or two, now and then.
And in the end I discovered what Michael really wanted
For making a new start. He wants to go abroad!
And find his own way in the world. That's very natural.
So I thought, why not appeal to Señor Gomez?
He's a wealthy man, and very important
In his own country. And a friend of Michael's father!
And I found him only too ready to help.

LORD CLAVERTON

And what was Señor Gomez able to suggest?

MRS. CARGHILL

Ah! That's the surprise for which I've come to prepare
   you.
Dear Michael is so happy—all his problems are solved;
And he was so perplexed, poor lamb. Let's all rejoice to-
   gether.
[*Enter* GOMEZ *and* MICHAEL]

LORD CLAVERTON

Well, Michael, you know I expected you this morning,
But you never came.

MICHAEL

No, Father. I'll explain why.

LORD CLAVERTON

And I learn that you have discussed your problems
With Mrs. Carghill and then with Señor Gomez.

113

MICHAEL

When I spoke, Father, of my wish to get abroad,
You couldn't see my point of view. What's the use of
    chasing
Half round the world, for the same sort of job
You got me here in London? With another Sir Alfred
Who'd constitute himself custodian of my morals
And send you back reports. Some sort of place
Where everyone would sneer at the fellow from London,
The limey remittance man for whom a job was made.
No! I want to go where I can make my own way,
Not merely be your son. That's what Señor Gomez sees.
He understands my point of view, if *you* don't.
And he's offered me a job which is just what I wanted.

LORD CLAVERTON

Yes, I see the advantage of a job created for you
By Señor Gomez . . .

MICHAEL

It's not created for me.
Señor Gomez came to London to find a man to fill it,
And he thinks I'm just the man.

GOMEZ

Yes, wasn't it extraordinary.

LORD CLAVERTON

Of course you're just the man that Señor Gomez wants,
But in a different sense, and for different reasons

From what you think. Let me tell you about Gomez.
He's unlikely to try to be custodian of your morals;
His real name is Culverwell . . .

GOMEZ
                               My dear Dick,
You're wasting your time, rehearsing ancient history.
Michael knows it already. I've told him myself.
I thought he'd better learn the facts from me
Before he heard your distorted version.
But, Dick, I was nettled by that insinuation
About my not being custodian of Michael's morals.
That is just what I should be! And most appropriate,
Isn't it, Dick, when we recall
That you were once custodian of *my* morals:
Though of course you went a little *faster* than I did.

LORD CLAVERTON
On that point, Fred, you're wasting *your* time:
My daughter and my future son-in-law
Understand that allusion. I have told them the story
In explanation of our . . . intimacy
Which they found puzzling.

MRS. CARGHILL
                       Oh, Richard!
Have you explained to them our intimacy too?

LORD CLAVERTON
I have indeed.

MRS. CARGHILL

The romance of my life.
Your father was simply *irresistible*
In those days. I melted the first time he looked at me!
Some day, Monica, I'll tell you all about it.

MONICA

I am satisfied with what I know already, Mrs. Carghill,
About you.

MRS. CARGHILL

But I was very lovely then.

GOMEZ

We are sure of that! You're so lovely now
That we can well imagine you at . . . what age were
    you?

MRS. CARGHILL

Just eighteen.

LORD CLAVERTON

Now, Michael,
Señor Gomez says he has told you his story.
Did he include the fact that he served a term in prison?

MICHAEL

He told me everything. It was his experience
With you, that made him so understanding
Of my predicament.

LORD CLAVERTON

And made him invent
The position which he'd come to find the man for.

MICHAEL

I don't care about that. He's offered me the job
With jolly good pay, and some pickings in commissions.
He's made a fortune there. San Marco for me!

LORD CLAVERTON

And what are your duties to be? Do you know?

MICHAEL

We didn't go into details. There's time for that later.

GOMEZ

Much better to wait until we get there.
The nature of business in San Marco
Is easier explained in San Marco than in England.

LORD CLAVERTON

Perhaps you intend to change your name to Gomez?

GOMEZ

Oh no, Dick, there are plenty of other good names.

MONICA

Michael, Michael, you can't abandon your family
And your very self—it's a kind of suicide.

CHARLES

Michael, you think Señor Gomez is inspired by benevo-
lence—

MICHAEL

I told you he'd come to London looking for a man
For an important post on his staff—

CHARLES

A post the nature of which is left very vague.

MICHAEL

It's confidential, I tell you.

CHARLES

So I can imagine:
Highly confidential . . .

GOMEZ

Be careful, Mr. Barrister.
You ought to know something about the law of slander.
Here's Mrs. Carghill, a reliable witness.

CHARLES

I know enough about the law of libel and slander
To know that you are hardly likely to invoke it.
And, Michael, here's another point to think of:
Señor Gomez has offered you a post in San Marco,
Señor Gomez pays your passage . . .

MICHAEL

And an advance of salary.

118

CHARLES

Señor Gomez pays your pasage . . .

GOMEZ

                              Just as many years ago
His father paid mine.

CHARLES

                    This return of past kindness
No doubt gives you pleasure?

GOMEZ

                         Yes, it's always pleasant
To repay an old debt. And better late than never.

CHARLES

I see your point of view. Can you really feel confidence,
Michael, in a man who aims to gratify, through you,
His lifelong grievance against your father?
Remember, you put yourself completely in the power
Of a man you don't know, of the nature of whose busi-
   ness
You know nothing. All you can be sure of
Is that he served a prison sentence for forgery.

GOMEZ

Well, Michael, what do you say to all this?

MICHAEL

I'll say that Hemington has plenty of cheek.
Señor Gomez and I have talked things over, Hemington . . .

GOMEZ

As two men of the world, we discussed things very
  frankly;
And I can tell you, Michael's head is well screwed on.
He's got brains, he's got flair. When he does come back
He'll be able to buy you out many times over.

MRS. CARGHILL

Richard, I think it's time *I* joined the conversation.
My late husband, Mr. Carghill, was a business man—
I wish you could have known him, Señor Gomez!
You're very much alike in some ways—
So I understand business. Mr. Carghill told me so.
Now, Michael has great abilities for business.
I saw that, and so does Señor Gomez.
He's simply been suffering, poor boy, from frustration.
He's been waiting all this time for opportunity
To make use of his gifts; and now, opportunity—
Opportunity has come knocking at the door.
Richard, you must not bar his way. That would be
  shameful.

LORD CLAVERTON

I cannot bar his way, as you know very well.
Michael's a free agent. So if he chooses
To place himself in your power, Fred Culverwell,
Of his own volition to contract his enslavement,
I cannot prevent him. I have something to say to you,
Michael, before you go. I shall never repudiate you
Though you repudiate me. I see now clearly

The many many mistakes I have made
My whole life through, mistake upon mistake,
The mistaken attempts to correct mistakes
By methods which proved to be equally mistaken.
I see that your mother and I, in our failure
To understand each other, both misunderstood you
In our divergent ways. When I think of your childhood,
When I think of the happy little boy who was Michael,
When I think of your boyhood and adolescence,
And see how all the efforts aimed at your good
Only succeeded in defeating each other,
How can I feel anything but sorrow and compunction?

MONICA

Oh Michael, remember, you're my only brother
And I'm your only sister. You never took much notice of
  me.
When we were growing up we seldom had the same
  friends.
I took all that for granted. So I didn't know till now
How much it means to me to have a brother.

MICHAEL

Why of course, Monica. You know I'm very fond of you
Though we never really seemed to have much in com-
  mon.
I remember, when I came home for the holidays
How it used to get on my nerves, when I saw you
Always sitting there with your nose in a book.
And once, Mother snatched a book away from you

And tossed it into the fire. How I laughed!
You never seemed even to want a flirtation,
And my friends used to chaff me about my highbrow
    sister.
But all the same, I was fond of you, and always shall be.
We don't meet often, but if we're fond of each other,
That needn't interfere with your life or mine.

MONICA

Oh Michael, you haven't understood a single word
Of what I said. You must make your own life
Of course, just as I must make mine.
It's not a question of your going abroad
But a question of the spirit which inspired your deci-
    sion:
If you wish to renounce your father and your family
What is left between you and me?

MICHAEL

                That makes no difference.
You'll be seeing me again.

MONICA

                But who will you be
When I see you again? Whoever you are then
I shall always pretend that it is the same Michael.

CHARLES

And when do you leave England?

MICHAEL

When we can get a passage.
And I must buy my kit. We're just going up to London.
Señor Gomez will attend to my needs for that climate.
And you see, he has friends in the shipping line
Who he thinks can be helpful in getting reservations.

MRS. CARGHILL

It's wonderful, Señor Gomez, how you manage *every-
thing!*
—No sooner had I put my proposal before him
Than he had it all planned out! It really was an inspira-
tion—
On my part, I mean. Are you listening to me, Richard?
You look very *distrait*. You ought to be excited!

LORD CLAVERTON

Is this good-bye then, Michael?

MICHAEL

Well, that just depends.
I could look in again. If there's any point in it.
Personally, I think that when one's come to a decision,
It's as well to say good-bye at once and be done with it.

LORD CLAVERTON

Yes, if you're going, and I see no way to stop you,
Then I agree with you, the sooner the better.
We may never meet again, Michael.

MICHAEL

I don't see why not.

GOMEZ

At the end of five years he will get his first leave.

MICHAEL

Well . . . there's nothing more to say, is there?

LORD CLAVERTON

Nothing at all.

MICHAEL

Then we might as well be going.

GOMEZ

Yes, we might as well be going.
You'll be grateful to me in the end, Dick.

MRS. CARGHILL

A parent isn't always the right person, Richard,
To solve a son's problems. Sometimes an outsider,
A friend of the family, can see more clearly.

GOMEZ

Not that I deserve any credit for it.
We can only regard it as a stroke of good fortune
That I came to England at the very moment
When I could be helpful.

MRS. CARGHILL

It's truly providential!

MONICA

Good-bye Michael. Will you let me write to you?

GOMEZ

Oh, I'm glad you reminded me. Here's my business card
With the full address. You can always reach him there.
But it takes some days, you know, even by air mail.

MONICA

Take the card, Charles. If I write to you, Michael,
Will you ever answer?

MICHAEL

Oh of course, Monica.
You know I'm not much of a correspondent;
But I'll send you a card, now and again,
Just to let you know I'm flourishing.

LORD CLAVERTON

Yes, write to Monica.

GOMEZ

Well, good-bye Dick. And good-bye Monica.
Good-bye, Mr. . . . Hemington.

MONICA

Good-bye Michael.
[*Exeunt* MICHAEL *and* GOMEZ]

125

Mrs. Carghill

I'm afraid this seems awfully sudden to you, Richard;
It isn't so sudden. We talked it all over.
But I've got a little piece of news of my own:
Next autumn, I'm going out to Australia,
On my doctor's advice. And on my way back
Señor Gomez has invited me to visit San Marco.
I'm so excited! But what pleases me most
Is that I shall be able to bring you news of Michael.
And now that we've found each other again,
We must always keep in touch. But you'd better rest
  now.
You're looking rather tired. I'll run and see them off.

[*Exit* Mrs. Carghill]

Monica

Oh Father, Father, I'm so sorry!
But perhaps, perhaps, Michael may learn his lesson.
I believe he'll come back. If it's all a failure
Homesickness, I'm sure, will bring him back to us;
If he prospers, that will give him confidence—
It's only self-confidence that Michael is lacking.
Oh Father, it's not you and me he rejects,
But himself, the unhappy self that he's ashamed of.
I'm sure he loves us.

Lord Claverton

Monica my dear,
What you say comes home to me. I fear for Michael;

126

Nevertheless, you are right to hope for something better.
And when he comes back, if he does come back,
I know that you and Charles will do what you can
To make him feel that he is not estranged from you.

CHARLES

We will indeed. We shall be ready to welcome him
And give all the aid we can. But it's both of you together
Make the force to attract him: you and Monica com-
bined.

LORD CLAVERTON

I shall not be here. You heard me say to him
That this might be a final good-bye.
I am sure of it now. Perhaps it is as well.

MONICA

What do you mean, Father? You'll be here to greet him.
But one thing I'm convinced of: you must leave Badgley
Court.

CHARLES

Monica is right. You should leave.

LORD CLAVERTON

This may surprise you: I feel at peace now.
It is the peace that ensues upon contrition
When contrition ensues upon knowledge of the truth.
Why did I always want to dominate my children?

127

Why did I mark out a narrow path for Michael?
Because I wanted to perpetuate myself in him.
Why did I want to keep you to myself, Monica?
Because I wanted you to give your life to adoring
The man that I pretended to myself that I was,
So that I could believe in my own pretences.
I've only just now had the illumination
Of knowing what love is. We all think we know,
But how few of us do! And now I feel happy—
In spite of everything, in defiance of reason,
I have been brushed by the wing of happiness.
And I am happy, Monica, that you have found a man
Whom you can love for the man he really is.

Monica

Oh Father, I've always loved you,
But I love you more since I have come to know you
Here, at Badgley Court. And I love you the more
Because I love Charles.

Lord Claverton

                   Yes, my dear.
Your love is for the real Charles, not a make-believe,
As was your love for me.

Monica

                   But not now, Father!
It's the real you I love—the man you are,
Not the man I thought you were.

128

                    And Michael—
I love him, even for rejecting me,
For the *me* he rejected, I reject also.
I've been freed from the self that pretends to be some-
        one;
And in becoming no one, I begin to live.
It is worth while dying, to find out what life is.
And I love you, my daughter, the more truly for know-
        ing
That there is someone you love more than your father—
That you love and are loved. And now that I love
        Michael,
I think, for the first time—remember, my dear,
I am only a beginner in the practice of loving—
Well, that is something.
                    I shall leave you for a while.
This is your first visit to us at Badgley Court,
Charles, and not at all what you were expecting.
I am sorry you have had to see so much of persons
And situations not very agreeable.
You two ought to have a little time together.
I leave Monica to you. Look after her, Charles,
Now and always. I shall take a stroll.

MONICA

At this time of day? You'll not go far, will you?
You know you're not allowed to stop out late
At this season. It's chilly at dusk.

Lord Claverton

Yes, it's chilly at dusk. But I'll be warm enough.
I shall not go far.

[*Exit* Claverton]

Charles

He's a very different man from the man he used to be.
It's as if he had passed through some door unseen by us
And had turned and was looking back at us
With a glance of farewell.

Monica

I can't understand his going for a walk.

Charles

He wanted to leave us alone together!

Monica

Yes, he wanted to leave us alone together.
And yet, Charles, though we've been alone to-day
Only a few minutes, I've felt all the time . . .

Charles

I know what you're going to say!
We *were* alone together, in some mysterious fashion,
Even with Michael, and despite those people,
Because somehow we'd begun to belong together,
And that awareness . . .

Monica

Was a shield protecting both of us . . .

130

CHARLES

So that now we are conscious of a new person
Who is you and me together.

                            Oh my dear,
I love you to the limits of speech, and beyond.
It's strange that words are so inadequate.
Yet, like the asthmatic struggling for breath,
So the lover must struggle for words.

MONICA

I've loved you from the beginning of the world.
Before you and I were born, the love was always there
That brought us together.

                          Oh Father, Father!
I could speak to you now.

CHARLES

                       Let me go and find him.

MONICA

We will go to him together. He is close at hand,
Though he has gone too far to return to us.
He is under the beech tree. It is quiet and cold there.
In becoming no one, he has become himself.
He is only my father now, and Michael's.
And I am happy. Isn't it strange, Charles,
To be happy at this moment?

CHARLES

                     It is not at all strange.
The dead has poured out a blessing on the living.

131

MONICA

Age and decrepitude can have no terrors for me,
Loss and vicissitude cannot appal me,
Not even death can dismay or amaze me
Fixed in the certainty of love unchanging.
                              I feel utterly secure
In you; I am a part of you. Now take me to my father.

CURTAIN

The Cast of the First Production
at the Edinburgh Festival
August 25—August 30, 1958

Monica Claverton-Ferry	ANNA MASSEY
Charles Hemington	RICHARD GALE
Lambert	GEOFFREY KERR
Lord Claverton	PAUL ROGERS
Federico Gomez	WILLIAM SQUIRE
Mrs. Piggott	DOROTHEA PHILLIPS
Mrs. Carghill	EILEEN PEEL
Michael Claverton-Ferry	ALEC McCOWEN

Presented by HENRY SHEREK
Directed by E. MARTIN BROWNE
Settings designed by HUTCHINSON SCOTT